THE MONSTER BOOK OF PICKLE JOKES

BEE BAILEY

Illustrated by
MARK EASTON

Purple Piglet Press

A division of Unitt Media, LLC

PO Box 191, Twisp, WA 98856

The Monster Book of Pickle Jokes

#1 in The Monster Book of Jokes Series

Coming Soon:

The Monster Book of Banana Jokes

The Monster Book of Chicken Jokes

The Monster Book of Dinosaur Jokes

Get more jokes and FREE STUFF at BeeBailey.com/pickles!

1

TASTY PICKLES

Q: Why did the pickle cross the road?
   A: To get to the other side dish.

Q: Where did the pickle go to have a few drinks?
   A: The salad bar.

Q: What did the pickle say when it found out it was going on a salad?

A: I relish the thought!

Q: How do cucumbers clean their teeth?

A: With a toothpickle.

Q: How do you make a pickle sundae?

A: By getting the ingredients ready on Friday and Saturday.

Q: What's a cucumber's favorite dessert?

A: Pickle brickle.

Q: Should you ever eat pickles on an empty stomach?

A: If you have to, but it's probably better to eat them on a plate.

Q: Is it proper to eat pickles with your fingers?

A: No, you should eat them separately.

Q: How do you turn a pickle into a squash?

A: Throw it in front of a bus.

Q: Why did the pickle climb up to the roof?
    A: It heard dinner was on the house.

Q: Why did the pickle wear red suspenders?
    A: The green ones were broken.

Q: Why are pickles so good?
    A: They can't help being dill-icious.

Q: Why is the pickle container always open?
    A: Because it's ajar.

Q: Is okay to eat pickles with fingers?
    A: Definitely not! Pickles should never have fingers.

Q: What happens when you get your hand stuck in the pickle jar?
    A: It's a real dill-emma.

Q: Why is the raspberry never in a pickle?
  A: I don't know, but it always seems to be in a jam!

Q: Why didn't the monster eat pickles?
  A: He couldn't fit his head in the jar.

Q: What do you call a frozen pickle?
  A: A pickle-sickle.

Q: What did the pickle think of the cucumbers?
  A: It thought they were dill-lightful.

Q: How do pickles cook their hot dogs?
  A: They grill them on the bar-b-cucumber.

Q: What's it called when you get to the very bottom of the pickle jar?
  A: Slim picklings.

Q: How do you make a pickle float?
  A: With two scoops of ice cream and some root beer.

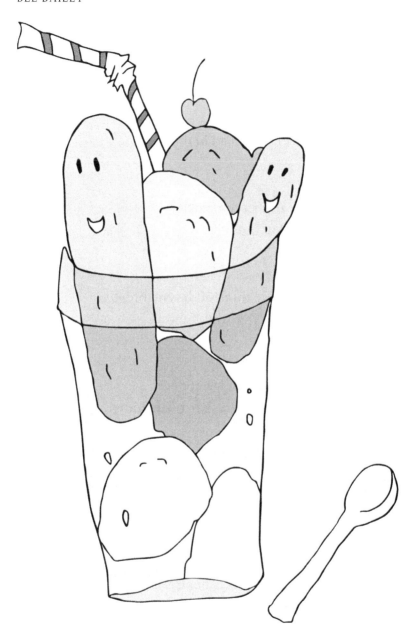

2

MUTANT PICKLES

Q : What's green and a hundred feet long?
A: A centipickle.

Q: What is green and has two wheels?
A: A motorpickle.

Q: What do you call a motorpickle with an extra seat?

A: A bipickle built for two.

Q: What do you get when you cross a pickle and a lizard?
   A: A crocodill.

Q: What is long and green and slimy and bumpy?
   A: A pick-eel.

Q: Who's the scariest pickle addict in the world?
   A: A one-eyed, one-horned, flying purple pickle eater.

Q: What's green, wears armor, and roams the streets of Texas?
   A: The arma-DILL-o.

Q: What's green, loud, and very, very dangerous?
   A: A thundering herd of pickles.

Q: What's green and sour and swims in an aquarium?
   A: A trop-pickle fish.

Q: What's green and goes slam, slam, slam, slam?
  A: A four-door pickle.

Q: What's green and goes click click?
  A: A ballpoint pickle.

Q: What's green, has 22 legs, and plays football in the snow?
  A: The Green Bay Pickles.

Q: What's green and roams the wilds of Africa?
  A: A picklepotamus.

3

LITTLE PICKLES

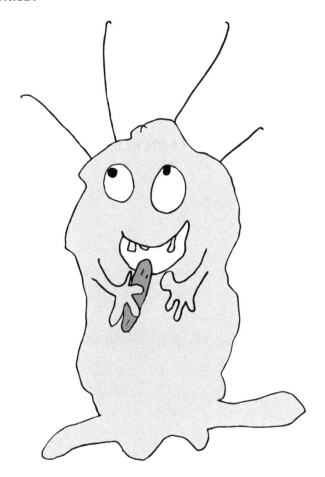

Q: Why do gherkins giggle a lot?
    A: They're picklish!

Q: Where do little pickles come from?
    A: A jar.

Q: What did the pickle yell at its misbehaving kids?
    A: Stop gherkin around!

Q: How do little pickles learn?
    A: With their brines.

Q: What's the baby cucumber's favorite toy?
    A: Pickle Me Elmo.

Q: Why did the little cucumbers like bobbing for pickles?
    A: Because it was a barrel of fun.

Q: If Santa married a pickle, what would they call their baby?
    A: Claussen.

Q: What do you do with pickles that are a year old?
    A: Wish them happy birthday!

Q: What does every little cucumber dream of?
    A: A cute little farmhouse with a white pickle fence.

Q: Which is the best cucumber in a batch of baby cucumbers?

A: The pickle the litter.

Q: What do little pickles put on their birthday cakes?

A: Canned dills.

Q: Why didn't the cucumbers like their teacher?

A: He nitpickled everything.

Q: What do you call a small sweet pickle that wears a vest?

A: A gherkin in a jerkin.

Q: What did the pickle say to the little cucumber?

A: Behold, your future!

Q: How did mama cucumber know her kids didn't feel well?

A: They didn't eat breakfast, they just pickled at it.

Q: What does the little pickle want to be when it grows up?

A: An Olympickle athlete.

Q: What TV station is preferred by little cucumbers everywhere?

A: Pickleodeon.

Q: What do you call a pickle lullaby?

A: A cucumber slumber number.

4

PICKLE FAVORITES

Q: What was the pickle's favorite kind of music?
   A: Vlasic rock.

Q: Who was the pickle's favorite pop star?
   A: Britney Spears.

Q: What was the Mexican pickle's favorite dance?

A: La Cuke-aracha.

Q: What is the pickle's favorite newspaper?
A: The Dilly Planet.

Q: What's the best motivational pickle book?
A: "How to Win Friends and Influence Pickles" by Dill Carnegie.

Q: Who was the pickle's favorite painter?
A: Salvador Dilly.

Q: What was the pickle's favorite Nancy Drew mystery?
A: The Secret of the Old Crock.

Q: What is the cucumber's favorite scary movie?
A: The Brining, starring Jack Pickleson.

Q: Who is the cucumber's favorite actor?
A: Pickle-us Cage.

Q: What was the cucumber's favorite spot in all of England?
   A: Pickle-dilly Circus.

Q: What's the pickle's favorite game show?
   A: Let's Make a Dill.

Q: What kind of books do pickles like?
   A: The spicy kind.

Q: What was the pickle's favorite color of crayon?
   A: Cuke umber.

Q: What's the pickle's favorite book?
   A: To Dill a Mockingbird.

Q: Where did the pickle want to go on vacation?
   A: To PhilaDILLphia.

Q: Who is grandma pickle's favorite singer?
   A: Elvis Pickley.

Q: Where do pickles love to go skiing?

A: Pike's Pickle.

5

PICKLE NONSENSE

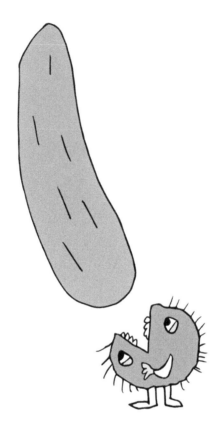

There was once a monster with a pickle in her ear.

Her friend said, "Hey, you've got a pickle in your ear!"

The monster took the pickle out of her ear and said, "Sorry, what did you say? I had a pickle in my ear."

DOCTOR: You must be very upset. There's a pickle growing out of your ear!

MONSTER: Of course I'm upset! I planted watermelon!

One pickle says to the other, "Why the sour face?"

The other one says, "I don't know, I'm just feeling a little green."

A monster was holding a jar of pickles and staring at it with a confused look on his face.

"What's wrong?" asked his friend.

"Well, it says to store these pickles in a cool, dark place."

"Okay, how about the fridge?"

"But there's a little light in there!"

I always get churros and pickles mixed up. It makes me chuckle.

Once there was a monster who was sitting by a very boring, flat river while eating a pickle. All at once, an idea came to him, and he threw the pickle in the river. Amazingly, the river transformed into a beautiful waterfall.

People came from miles around to see the miracle waterfall.

"How did you know to toss the pickle in the river?" they asked.

"Oh," said the monster, "I just thought of that old saying, 'Dill waters run steep!'"

MONSTER 1: Hey, why is there a pickle behind your ear?

MONSTER 2: Oh dear, I must have eaten my pencil for lunch!

Words that rhyme with pickle:
tickle
brickle
sickle
fickle
nickel
icicle
bicycle
bananapickle

That pickle sure is fickle. Yesterday it was a cucumber; today it thinks it's a big dill!

Janie Monster works at a pickle factory. She is 5'6" tall, with brown hair and brown eyes. What does she weigh?

Pickles, of course!

WARNING: Pickles can kill you. The long-term effects of

eating pickles are deadly: 100% of people who ate pickles before 1898 are now dead!

In spite of the overwhelming evidence, the pickle industry continues to thrive.

We recommend eating chocolate chip cookies instead. They are much safer than pickles.

A monster goes to the doctor's office with a carrot poking out of his eye, a pickle stuck inside his nose, and a banana in his ear.

The doctor takes one look and says, "Nurse! This monster hasn't been eating properly!"

MONSTER: Doctor, my skin seems to have turned green and bumpy! Is that normal?

DOCTOR: Well, it isn't typickle.

I opened a jar of pickles once. It only took me 20 minutes and a hammer.

6

FAMOUS PICKLES

Q : What's green and says, "oink oink"?
A: Porky Pickle.

Q: What's green and hairy and hangs out in New York?
    A: King Kong Pickle.

Q: What's green and swims in the sea?
    A: Moby Pickle.

Q: What's green and wears a mask?
    A: The Lone Pickle.

Q: What's green and pecks on trees?
    A: Woody Wood Pickle.

Q: What's green and walks thru walls?
    A: Casper the Friendly Cucumber.

Q: Who's the jolly cucumber that brings presents to all the good little pickles?
    A: St. Pickle-us.

Q: What's the name of the pickle vampire?
    A: Count Vat-ula. And all he drinks is pickle juice.

Q: What's green and flies through the air?
   A: Superpickle!

7

PICKLES AT WORK

Q : Why did the cucumber need a lawyer?
A: Because it was in a pickle.

Q: What did the pickle salesman say?

A: Have I got a dill for you!

Q: Why was the pickle dentist sued?

A: For dilling the wrong tooth.

Q: What is the difference between a pickle and a psychiatrist?

A: If you don't know, you should probably stop talking to your pickle.

Q: How did the smart business pickle make its millions?

A: It opened a dill-icatessen.

Q: Why did the cucumber have such good luck?

A: It was all due to the pickle finger of fate.

Q: What did the boss pickle say to cheer up its workers?

A: That's the spear-it!

Q: What do you call a pickle you buy on sale?

A: A sweet dill.

Q: What did the Russian pickle paint on the wall of its deli?
    A: A hammer and a pickle.

Q: What do cowboy cucumbers drive?
    A: Pickleup trucks.

Q: What did the pickle say to Congress?
    A: Nothing. Pickles can't talk!

Q: What do you call a pickle doctor?
    A: A dill pusher.

Q: Where do pickles go when they're sick?
    A: The vat-rinarian.

Q: Who's the richest pickle in the world?
    A: A pickle with a nickel.

Q: Why are cucumbers always late?
    A: They like to DILLydally.

Q: Why couldn't the pickles get to work on time?

   A: Because they were always in a crunch.

Q: Why couldn't the farmer afford to stop growing cucumbers?

   A: They were his bread and butter.

Q: What did the doctor prescribe for the pickle's itchy skin?

   A: A topickle ointment.

Q: How do pickles go on strike?

   A: They form pickle lines.

8

COLORFUL PICKLES

Q: What's black and white and green all over?
A: The pickle that fell into the printer.

Q: What is black and white and green and grumpy?
A: A sour pickle in a tuxedo.

Q: What's black and white and black and white and black and white and green?
A: Three zebras fighting over a pickle.

Q: What's black and white and green and black and white?
A: Two penguins fighting over a pickle.

Q: Why was the cucumber looking so rosy?
A: It was pickled pink.

Q: What's green and green and squishy and green?
A: A pickle rolling down the stairs.

Q: What's red and white and green and stuck in the chimney?
A: Santa Claus in a pickle.

Q: If you throw a green pickle into the Red Sea, what does it become?

A: Wet.

Q: What is green and travels through steel?
A: A pickle, but only if you throw it very hard!

Q: What's green and white and green and white and green?
A: A pickle making snow angels.

Q: What's green and yellow and green and yellow and green?
A: A pickle that works as a banana impersonator.

Q: How do you make a green pickle?
A: Cross a blue pickle with a yellow one.

Q: What's green and red all over?
A: A sunburned pickle.

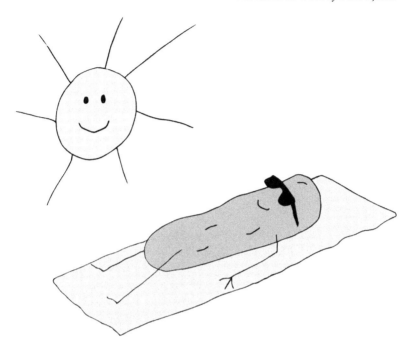

9

PICKLED RELATIONSHIPS

Q : What did the stuck up pickle say?
A: I'm kind of a big dill.

Q: Why are pickles lousy friends?
A: They're always green with envy.

Q: Why are sandwich pickles so polite?
    A: They're well bread.

Q: Why was one pickle bored with the other?
    A: The other was getting very dill.

Q: Why did the pickle shut its eyes?
    A: It saw the salad dressing!

Q: What did the big pickle say to the little pickle who failed a test?
    A: Don't worry, it's no big dill.

Q: What did the mean pickle say when it stole the little pickle's lunch money?
    A: Dill with it.

Q: What did the pickle say to its best friend?
    A: You mean a great dill to me!

Q: What do you call a pickle who's a bad loser?
    A: A sour pickle.

Q: What did one dill say to the other dill?
 A: Well this is a fine pickle you got us into!

Q: Why did the dating pickles break up?
 A: They soured on each other.

Q: What's the first line at a pickle wedding?
 A: Dilly beloved...

Q: What was in the pickle's wedding bouquet?
 A: Roses and dillies.

Q: What did the sweet pickle say to the love of its life?
 A: Pucker up!

Q: What did the mother pickle say to her teenage son?
 A: You're getting mixed up in something sour, and I don't like it!

Q: What did the teenage pickle say to his mother?

A: Please, mom, spear me.

Q: What did the pickle say to the hot dog?
   A: I relish this time we have together.

10

KNOCK KNOCK

K nock knock!
        Who's there?
Pickle!
Pickle who?
Pickle little flower for me, would you?

Knock knock!
>Who's there?
>Pickle!
>Pickle who?
>This isn't a piccolo, it's a trombone!

Knock! Knock!
>Who's there?
>This pickle!
>This pickle who?
>This pick'll break a rock into smithereens!

Knock! Knock!
>Who's there?
>Pickle!
>Pickle who?
>Pickle someone your own size!

Knock knock!
>Who's there?
>Pickle!
>Pickle who?
>Pickle this lock if you don't open the door!

Knock! Knock!

Who's there?
Pickle!
Pickle who?
Pickle letter from A-Z.
(they pick a letter)
Do you know what letter cucumbers always pick?
No, what?
They always pick 'L.'"

Knock knock!
Who's there?
A pickle juice!
A pickle juice who?
Gesundheit!

11

YOU'LL BE PICKLED PINK

Q : What is the pickle philosophy of life?
A: Never a dill moment!

Q: What do you call the pickle that got run over on the highway?

A: Road dill.

Q: What do you call frozen pickles hanging from the roof?
A: Icepickles.

Q: Why shouldn't you use a pickle as a pool cue?
A: You'll find the cue cumbersome.

Q: What do you do when a pickle wants to play cards?
A: Dill 'em in.

Q: Why did the fruit fly dance on the pickle jar?
A: Because it said "twist to open."

Q: What happens when you get vinegar in your ear?
A: You suffer from pickled hearing.

Q: What do you call a cucumber that was attacked by a bird?
A: A peckled pickle.

Q: Why did the cucumber stop rolling down the hill?
   A: Because it ran out of pickle juice.

Q: How do pickles enjoy a nice picnic?
   A: They relish it.

Q: What did the skeptical pickle say?
   A: Quit gherkin my chain.

Q: What did the hipster pickle say?
    A: What's the dilly-yo?

Q: Why did the cucumber check into the hospital?
    A: For a cure.

Q: What do you call a pickle that runs back and forth all day long?
    A: A willy-nilly dilly, or a fickle pickle!

Q: What do you call a pickle from the backwoods?
    A: A hill-dilly.

Q: Why don't cucumbers like being turned into pickles?
    A: It's just too jarring.

Q: How do you prevent bumps on a pickle?
    A: Cover it with mosquito repellent.

Q: What do you call a thieving cucumber?
    A: A picklepocket.

Q: How do you hunt wild cucumbers?
   A: With a spear gun.

Q: What did one cucumber seed say to the other?
   A: We're really in a pickle!

Q: How did the cucumber figure out who was the impostor?
   A: One was just a pickle, but the other was the real dill.

Q: How does a pickle yodel?
   A: Oh-dill-aye-hee-hoo!

Q: How do you spell pickle backwards?
   A: P-i-c-k-l-e b-a-c-k-w-a-r-d-s

Q: Why are we telling you all these pickle jokes?
   A: Kosher such a nice person!

Q: How can you tell when there are 1,000 pounds of pickles under your bed?
   A: You're much closer to the ceiling!

12

PICKLE WORDS

"You're looking a little green..."

Not sure what some of the words mean? Don't be sour, keep reading!

Pickle *(noun)* – a cucumber that has been preserved through a process called pickling

Pickle *(verb)* – to preserve food using salt water or vinegar

Brine – very salty water; used to make some kinds of pickles

Vat – a large tank used to prepare foods

Kosher pickles – pickles with a strong flavor, made with lots of garlic and dill

Pickle chips – pickles that are cut crosswise into round slices; often used on hamburgers

Spears – pickles that are cut lengthwise, like long spears

Gherkins – small cucumbers that make small pickles, about the size of a baby carrot

Relish – a condiment made from finely chopped pickles; often served on hot dogs

Ferment – to change chemically because of yeast or bacteria

Curing – a way to preserve food by letting it age in salt, sugar, vinegar, or smoke

Dill – an herb used to flavor pickles; also the name of the most popular flavor of pickle

Bread and Butter – a type of sweet pickle

Claussen, Vlasic – popular pickle manufacturers

13

PICKLE FACTS

I know what a pickle is, but what exactly IS a pickle?

A pickle is a cucumber that has been "pickled."

Pickling is a way to keep food from spoiling.

Foods are put into vinegar or brine (salt water). When the liquid soaks through the food, it is "cured" and ready to eat.

The acid in the liquid kills bad bacteria, so the food does not spoil.

People have been preserving food this way for thousands of years, but you probably don't want to eat a thousand-year old pickle!

"I hope this pickle isn't a thousand years old. I should've checked the expiration date..."

What kinds of foods can be pickled?

Almost any food can be pickled, but most pickled foods fall into three groups:

Vegetables – cucumbers, peppers, onions, beets, carrots, cabbage, green beans, etc.

Fruits – plums, apples, pears, peaches, etc.

Proteins – fish, tofu, beef, eggs, etc.

Even though many foods can be pickled, only pickled cucumbers are called "pickles."

"I prefer pickled plums, pickled peaches, and pickled parsnips. Positively."

How are pickles made?

There are three ways to make pickles:

REFRIGERATOR PICKLES
Cucumbers are put in vinegar and spices, then refrigerated.
Once the liquid soaks in, the pickles are ready to eat.

These pickles are extra crispy and have a short shelf life.

FRESH PACK PICKLES
Cucumbers are put in vinegar and spices, then heated.

These pickles are usually crispier and less sour than
processed pickles.

PROCESSED PICKLES (AKA FERMENTED PICKLES)
Cucumbers are put into vats of brine, where they ferment
for a few months. When they are ready, the pickles are
rinsed, packed in jars, and seasoning is added.

These pickles have a tangy flavor.

"I heard that Peter Piper picked a peck of pickled peppers."

What are the different flavors of pickles?

Dill Pickles

Dill pickles are the most popular kind of pickle. They get most of their flavor from an herb called dill, but there are many different flavors of dill pickles:

Genuine dills are made using the processed method. They are more sour than other dills.

German dills are made using vinegar. They are less sour than other dills.

Kosher dills are made with lots of garlic. Many people find this type of pickle delicious!

Polish dills use lots of garlic and spices, and tend to be hot or peppery.

SOUR PICKLES

Sour pickles are made with brine, not vinegar. The longer the pickles sit in the salty brine, the more sour they become.

Sour pickles come in sour and half-sour. Half sour pickles use less salt and do not soak as long.

Sweet Pickles

Sweet pickles are made with sugar. There are several types of sweet pickles:

Bread and butter pickles have a tangy flavor. They are usually cut in thin slices and used in sandwiches and hamburgers.

Candied pickles are packed in syrupy liquid, so they are extra-sweet.

Kool-Aid pickles (aka koolickles) are soaked in Kool-Aid.

This makes them both sweet and sour. These pickles are also brightly colored, depending on the flavor of Kool-Aid.

What are the most popular pickles?

Dill pickles, with sweet pickles in second place.

Are pickles good for you?

Yes! They are fat free and have very few calories. They do contain a lot of salt, though, so you probably shouldn't eat too many.

"They better be good for me. They're all I eat!"

How many pickles are eaten every year?

In the United States, about 20 billion pickles are eaten every year. That's about 63 pickles per person each year.

More than 67% of U.S. households eat pickles. On average, they buy pickles every 53 days.

"That's nothing. I can eat 63 pickles in a day!"

How did the pickle get its name?

Some people think the word "pickle" came from the Dutch word "pekel," meaning brine.

Others believe the word came from saying the name of Mr. William Beukelz wrong. In the 1300's, Mr. Beukelz was known for making pickled fish.

How big was the world's largest pickle?

Unfortunately, nobody has been measuring giant pickles, but we do know a little bit about cucumbers.

According to the Guinness Book of World Records, the longest cucumber ever recorded was 42.1 inches (107 cm) long, and was grown by Ian Neale of Wales in 2011.

The heaviest cucumber was 23 lbs. 7 oz. (12.9 kg), and was grown by Dave Thomas from England in 2015.

There must be something in the water in the United Kingdom!

Recently, Daniel Tomelin from Canada said that he grew a 44.5 inch (113 cm) long cucumber. He planned to turn it into the world's longest pickle.

Where is the biggest pickle factory in the world?

Holland, Michigan. The H. J. Heinz Company opened a pickle factory there in 1898, and it is still running today.

How many pickles would it take to stretch around the world? To reach the moon?

About 417 million pickles to stretch around the world, and 4 billion to get to the moon.

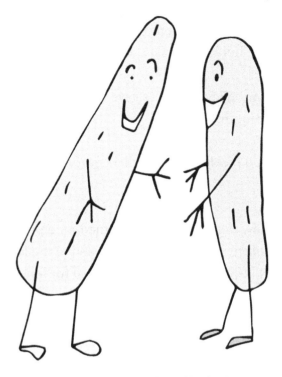

"The moon? But I'm afraid of heights."

Famous People and Pickles

Elvis Presley loved fried pickles.

The hosts of NBC's Late Night talk show each inherit a giant plastic pickle. First it belonged to David Letterman, who passed it to Conan O'Brien, who passed it to Jimmy Fallon, who passed it to Seth Meyers.

Cleopatra, a ruler of ancient Egypt, thought that eating pickles made her beautiful.

Julius Caesar believed pickles gave his soldiers physical and spiritual strength.

Napoleon fed pickles to his soldiers every day to keep them healthy.

Did you know that America was named for a pickle peddler? Before Amerigo Vespucci sailed to the New World, he sold pickles in Spain. Pickles are good for long voyages, because they don't spoil easily and they are full of Vitamin C.

Queen Elizabeth I, George Washington, Dolly Madison, and Thomas Jefferson all loved pickles.

Miscellaneous Pickle Facts

Americans prefer their pickles with bumps; Europeans prefer them without.

International Pickle Week takes place during the last two weeks of May. (Why isn't it called International Pickle Two Weeks?)

During World War II, the U.S. Government kept 40% of the nation's pickles for soldiers' meals.

You should be able to hear a good pickle crunch from 10 steps away.

Find more pickle facts at:

Pickle Packers International, ilovepickles.org
NY Food Museum, nyfoodmuseum.org

14

MAKE YOUR OWN PICKLES

D id you know you can make pickles at home? Here is an easy recipe for you to try, with help from your favorite grown up.

Easy Refrigerator Pickles

- *6 small cucumbers*
- *1 tablespoon dried dill*
- *1 clove garlic, peeled and crushed*
- *1 tablespoon pickling salt, kosher salt, or sea salt (do not use iodized table salt)*
- *1 cup apple cider vinegar*
- *1 cup water*

1. Cut cucumbers into spears or rounds. Place into a clean quart-sized jar. Add the dill and garlic.
2. In a glass bowl, combine salt, vinegar, and water. Stir until the salt is dissolved.
3. Pour salt water mixture over the cucumbers, until the jar is full.
4. Place lid on jar and refrigerate for at least 3 days before eating. Keep refrigerated.

For crunchier pickles, use cucumbers that are firm and dark green.

Once you have eaten all the pickles, save the juice for another batch of pickles. Just add more cucumbers, let sit for 3 days, and enjoy more pickles!

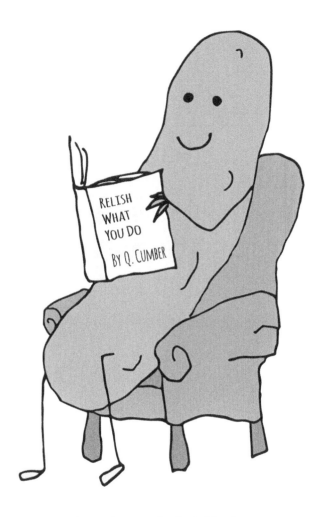

Q: Where is the best place to find pickles?
    A: Right where you left them.

Looking for more monstrously good jokes?

Visit <u>BeeBailey.com/pickles</u> for more jokes and
FREE STUFF!

"I love free stuff! Don't you?"